To she

My Insp

Love you Always

Mummy x

101 Days of

Inspiration

#TipoftheDay

101 Days of

Inspiration

#TipoftheDay

Susan Leigh

Published in 2016 by

Stellar Books LLP
39 Eyebrook Road
Bowdon
Cheshire
WA14 3LQ, UK.

E: info@stellarbooks.co.uk
W: www.stellarbooks.co.uk
T: 0161 928 8273
Tw: @stellarbooksllp

ISBN: 978-1-910275-16-0

A copy of this book is available in the British Library.

Copyright © Susan Leigh 2016

Typeset by Stellar Books

• • •

This book is dedicated to my late husband Frederick Leigh and to my support team who provide a miscellany of inspiration, encouragement and cocktails.
Thank you.

Books by Susan Leigh

Dealing with Death, Coping with the Pain

Dealing with Stress, Managing its Impact

101 Days of Inspiration #TipoftheDay

Introduction

Many of us will have had occasions when we've read something thought-provoking or overheard a snatch of conversation that's stayed with us, causing us to stop and reflect for a little while.

The aim of this book is to provide a regular interlude for you in your busy days, ways to enjoy 'ah ha' moments and daily inspiration.

Based on my popular '#tipoftheday' on social media this collection of 101 reflections is able to be used at the beginning of each day as a mini-meditation, or it can be taken with you and dipped into throughout the course of the day, as you wish.

Enjoy each opportunity to make the most of these moments and commit to live life well.

Do you make resolutions at the

beginning of the year?

Whilst New Year can be a good time to reflect on
your life and the direction you're going in, **any**
day can be a good day to start anew.
Are you simply drifting along, aimlessly
following whichever tide flows your way or
are you actually giving real consideration
and input to what happens!
Set yourself valid, viable goals at

any time of the year!

Avoid the early year lethargy, that end of January/early February National Sickie Day inertia when many people feel overwhelmed and fed up with their debt, job, life or the miserable weather!

Find ways to plan something to look forward to, b r e a k the routine and add a little colour to your life.

Avoid those post-Christmas blues.

— ❧❦❧ —

Remember that 'yes' can be the most

- negative - word in your vocabulary

and 'no' can be the most

+ positive +!

Use both with thought as to the consequences!

Today's a **gift,**
that's why it's called
the **present.**
Enjoy your gift and relish even
the mundane.
Someone else could well be
thrilled
to be in your shoes.

—— ⁙ ——

Enjoy keeping a life diary, a journal of the significant events each year; anniversaries, exams passed, events attended.

It's SO easy to forget key moments.
This way, at the end of each year
you can reminisce on how much has
happened throughout the year.

—— ❦ ——

Learn from failure and understand what went wrong so that you don't repeat the same ~~misteaks~~ mistakes. But also monitor and learn from your successes too.

By paying attention
to what worked well you can be
sure to repeat it again!

• • •

Enjoy that first hour in the morning.

It's often time when there's clearer thinking

and can be a great time to write,

practise yoga, go for a run or drive unhindered

by traffic, resulting in your adopting a

calmer approach to life.

Really successful people

often relish getting up early to work

on their plans for the day in order

to be in a 'good place' mentally.

Difficulty sleeping can be caused by being too warm rather than too cold.
Make sure your bedroom is properly aired and ventilated; then prepare to settle down comfortably.

How do you feel when things don't go to plan? Know that some of the greatest successes have evolved from things that didn't work out as intended! Use what you've got!

Ask others for help; you'll be surprised how often people are thrilled to be included and may even be able to contribute some great, unexpected ideas!

Today's thought for the day is on Death and Dying.

*For those dying, it's often a source of comfort to
be given permission to let go and no longer
need to fight to stay alive.
People who are dying can have serious concerns
about how those left behind will cope, whether
they'll be able to carry on without them.
Reassurance about this can provide great relief.*

*Allow those you love to make their transition in
peace and comfort, as much as they possibly can.*

*This is something you can do with your
beloved animals too.*

Have you heard of a safari supper? Everyone prepares a course and walks from one house to the next as the meal progresses; it can be an inexpensive, less onerous way to entertain whilst getting to know your neighbours.

How often are we full of good intentions,
a real desire to make changes and
improvements to our lives and then,
just as easily, that positive
mind-set goes, vanishing into thin air!
Monitor your results, be answerable
to someone else or give
yourself rewards along the way.
Find something that keeps you motivated!

—— ⸎⸎⸎⸎ ——

Every year there's an International Day of
Happiness, the objective being to find a positive
outlook on life, treat ourselves well and
count our blessings!
Why not treat each day as such and enjoy
today being Happiness Day!

• • •

Weekends can sometimes end up a bit random,
so that by Sunday evening we find ourselves
feeling a bit irritated that we didn't make plans
to catch up with an important friend, go for a walk
in the countryside, visit the beach, spend
30 minutes dealing with a messy work thing or
have some 'me time' with a book.

Decide to remedy that this weekend.

A little forethought can improve the quality
of your weekends and make them much
more positive for you!

Whilst getting from A to B

is important

don't forget to enjoy the journey

and relish the opportunities for

occasional detours;

they can provide fabulous adventures,

new direction and unexpected

enhancements to your life.

There's no long term advantage to working unremittingly. Find ways to incorporate stress-busting activities into your daily life and routine.

Breaks, fun and 'me time' are all ways to disengage for a while and give yourself time to switch off.

You'll find that you return to work feeling refreshed and often with a better outlook on the task in hand.

PERFORMANCE
MANAGEMENT
scope
job critical
overruns
improvement
commitment
priorities
intervenes
benefits
workforce
results
rewarded
efficiency
monitored
surveys
scenario
enhanced
discrepancy
recording
correlation
unlocking
reporting
problem
strategic
set
notes
work
development
fail
directly
time
appraisal
management
statement

Stories are a **great** way
to convey information
as they operate on many levels: factual,
emotional, and by tapping into personal &
historical references within people's lives.

Some people value children's stories;
The Ugly Duckling is a great one for reflecting
on how beautiful being different often is.

Other people use inspirational stories about
themselves or their clients and customers.

Consider how stories can work
well for you.

Many people ~~delete~~ *names off
their lists or periodically clear
out their address books, but
what about those 'friends' who
clutter our lives,
consume the little free time
we can't afford to waste and
cause stress rather than pleasure.*

*Sometimes
we need to de-clutter people
from our lives too.*

Many people have an extra day off work over Bank Holiday weekends. Ensure that you allow even a small window of time for something that really makes you smile, be proud or think 'Well done'.

Today's not a dress rehearsal;
give each moment your full
attention! Rather than mull over
the past or become preoccupied
about the future.
Stay with the here and now.
That's all we have.

Millions

of working days each

year are lost due to stress.

Become familiar with your

'amber lights',

those warning signs that let you know

things are becoming too much!

How **wonderful** to be able to say

'I planted that, look how *beautiful* it's become'.

Enjoy watching your seeds and plants grow,

but don't forget to weed, water and tend them!

Even if they don't grow as well you'd hoped,

learn from the experience and treat it as great

practice for the future. And remember that

weeds often have their own beauty.

When rain and thunderstorms are

predicted do you say,

'WHAT a horrible day'

or simply view it as one where it's

raining a lot?

Perspective is the key!

When you hear that

45 million

days have been lost this past 3 years due to stress
or that 90% of adults say they don't get enough
sleep it's no wonder that people look for ways
to improve their ability to cope.

Take regular breaks, eat as healthily as you
can and try to schedule some

'me time'

for exercise, fun, reading a good book
or simply relaxing.

When you shop you're not interested in everything that's on offer - neither are your clients and customers.

Listen carefully when they come to do business with you so that you can demonstrate respect for their needs and time.

Get to know them better, then you'll be able to occasionally offer them something extra that would add value to their business.

How do you keep the spark in your relationship with your partner? A survey reveals that we spend up to £250,000 over the years on gifts, say 'I love you' 16 times a month, enjoy 1 holiday and 2-3 mini-breaks a year without the children. Maintaining the spark, though, requires the important touches, being thoughtful and attentive all the time, not just on special occasions!

What are the

BEST

moments of your life?
Remind yourself of what's possible and

enjoy the journey.

— ❧ —

Did you know that 1 in 5 people work at least
7 hours a week in unpaid overtime?
And that doesn't include the self-employed and
small business owners who often invest much of
themselves and their time into keeping their
businesses afloat.

But it does beg the question, is work too
important in your life?

Might it be time to reorder your priorities?

Just reflecting on how we so easily discard things when they're broken. We treat old, tattered possessions with disdain, not looking to fix, repair or make do. And equally, if we're feeling low, damaged or broken we may be ashamed, even contemptuous.

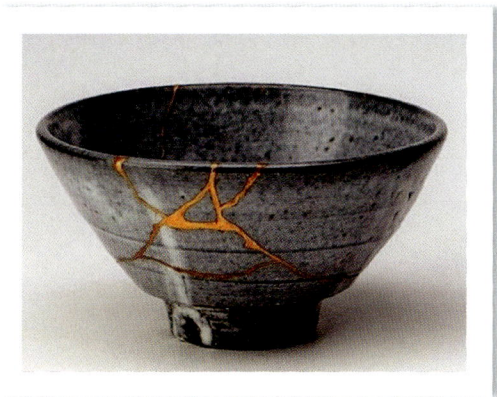

Have you heard of the Japanese method (Kintsugi) of fixing broken china, bowls and pots by pouring liquid gold into the cracks? Those healed pots are at their strongest and most beautiful in the areas that were once damaged.

Women apparently lose

8 hours

a month deciding what to wear!
The vicissitudes of the weather can make it
tough to decide each morning, as can the varied
demands of each day. Putting clothes out the
night before, layering when you dress so that
items can be added or removed, or even
having a work 'uniform' of a particular
colour or style can all help to minimise the
pressure of what to wear.

———— ⚜ ————

*Learn from failure but also learn
from success too – repeat what works
and let it become a
part of your approach to life!*

• • •

Even on the darkest of days get into the habit of finding 3 things that went well.

It might be an unexpected gesture or phone call that made you smile, a child's laughter in the park or that you felt better once you'd made the effort

to sort a problem.

<u>DETERMINE</u> to leave that dark place.

Don't just hand out business cards like confetti.
Build relationships and get to know, like and trust each other. Human connections are the key to solid business growth!

— ⚜ —

Are you surprised when people misunderstand you or appear oblivious of your tastes, likes and dislikes? Improve your relationships by listening and communicating properly, by being open, honest and respectful.

Look how beautiful
a heart that's been
broken can become.

It was exhilarating to watch the 35,000
runners in the Manchester 10k
help and support each other to
the finish line.
A common goal provides an arena in
which to share energy and motivate
each other to succeed.

— ～◦◦◦◦◦～ —

*Consider how your genius can also
be your curse!
Be careful about bringing home perfectionism,
attention to detail or serious
organisational and
time management skills.*

What about your image, how you
come across to others?
Invest in a key piece, a smart tie or piece
of jewellery, a nice haircut and give
your look a boost.

P-a-u-s-e and celebrate your
★ successes.

People enjoy being included in your good news.

Share your good results stories.

*Exercise doesn't have to be a chore.
Why not go for a walk with a friend or
loved one? You could put the meal in the
oven to slowly cook and be greeted
upon your return by a delicious meal
that's ready to be enjoyed.*

How are you with compliments? It's important to accept praise and appreciation with a good grace. Try smiling or saying a simple, 'Thank you'.

Be considerate to the giver and let them feel good too.

*I read somewhere that a happy client or customer will tell **four** people, whilst an unhappy one will tell **eleven**.*

It's important to keep ensuring that you have lots of happy clients who continue to share your name with their four contacts!!

Incredibly, a reported 25% of adults have insomnia on a Sunday night! No wonder Mondays are often so tough, with any worries compounded by lack of proper sleep!
Maybe 30 minutes spent planning the coming week could help alleviate some of the worry, resulting in a better sense of being in control of your time.

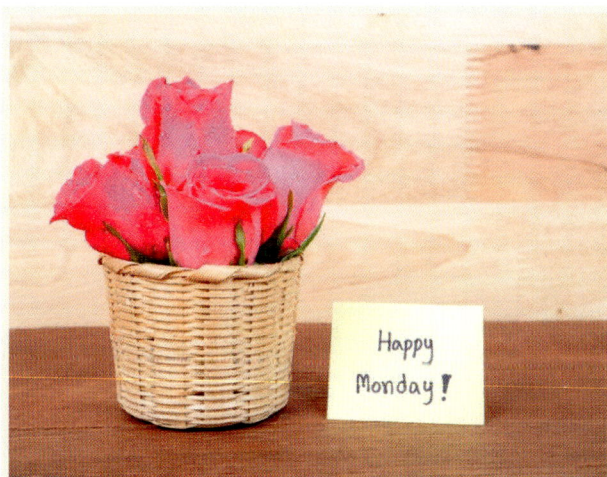

Let others choose to buy rather than try to
sell to them! Consistently demonstrate
how good you are; then they'll sing
your praises and ask to
trade with you!

— ⟋⟍ ❧ ⟋⟍ —

*Lots of people sell what you do; set yourself
apart by establishing a special likeable edge,
something that elevates you above your
competition.*

— ⟋⟍ ❧ ⟋⟍ —

Don't give to get.
Be generous with time, recommendations
and acts of kindness.
Rewards often come when you
least expect them.

• • •

Do you say 'sorry' automatically, without even thinking? Many of us do but sorry infers 'I'm in the wrong, I'm at fault'. When you apologise be clear about what and why you're sorry. Might it be that you needed to say or do what you did but are sorry at the upset it caused. Apologise for that: 'It wasn't my intention to upset you; I'm sorry that it caused you distress.'

Some people are 'old' at 30.
Others are 'young' at 80.
Why not choose your age and
decide to

LIVE LIFE WELL

— ✥ —

90% of disagreements are caused about our sleeping habits. Snoring, hogging the bed covers, reading, TV and eating in bed can all require some compromise!

Find solutions that suit you both.

Do you stop yourself from asking for what you want or simply expect others to know intuitively?

*Speak up and say what you feel,
ask for what you need and
give others the opportunity to treat
you how you want to be treated.
Respect your relationships.*

Try to allow time to literally appreciate where you are; look up, enjoy the views, the architecture, your town, the ways it's changing. It's so easy to rush unseeing from place to place when you're busy and that can become a habit!

Give to charity;

whether it be time, effort or money, find a charity that has meaning for you and reinvest something of yourself back into the world.

Share an hour or two with friends or neighbours and get to know them better. Organise a game of football or cricket and share exercise and fun as you all get fitter together.

You've finished your list of chores
and obligations.
Don't you feel fab when
you've a few moments
grace and can
relax over the newspapers.

How do you react when someone has an opposing opinion or disagrees with you? Be interested and listen to an alternative perspective.

It can be a revelation to discover a different way of looking at things.

Delegate tasks to your children, partner or staff.
It may take time for them to become adept
but learning new skills allows them to grow in
confidence and gain pleasure from becoming more
responsible and involved, to be enthusiastic
about working together.

— ❦ —

Occasionally revisit basic training.
It can be good to be reminded of old skills
that can be used in new and different
ways or reintroduce forgotten or discarded
techniques. Seize opportunities to
occasionally refresh 'old' skills and
use them in innovative ways.

• • •

When you're enjoying a lovely 3 day Bank
Holiday with an extra day off work, plan for
family time, with maybe some time for work, but
don't forget to include a little 'me time' as well.
Then when Tuesday arrives feel good that you've
used your extra time well.

— ❦ —

In what ways have you or your business
changed over the years?
Reflect on how far you've come,
the lessons learned and where you
want to be in the future.

Enjoy each opportunity to g r o w!

— ❦ —

• • •

Sleep is like a little kitten;
try to grab it and it will run away
and elude you.
Be still and let it settle,
then it will come to you naturally.

———— ❦ ————

How often do you agree to something and
then end up feeling

resentful, irritated or angry?

Learn not to agree to things automatically,
out of guilt or for an easy life.
Be honest and make for a better
atmosphere in the long term!

Expect something to be good or bad, easy or
tough and you'll approach it accordingly!
Change your mind-set and see how often

+++ positive +++

results follow through.

Allow even a small window of time
today and do something that
really makes you smile, feel proud
or think to yourself,

'Well done!'

Give some advance thought to your coming
weekend's entertainment and activities
then you don't waste half of your weekend
in deliberations and discussions!

Drop the word 'networking' if it sounds

daunting. Instead chat, ask people

questions and express interest in

helping them succeed.

You'll build relationships and be

remembered in a positive way.

Everyone has something to offer. Listen, ask questions and discover the gems around you.

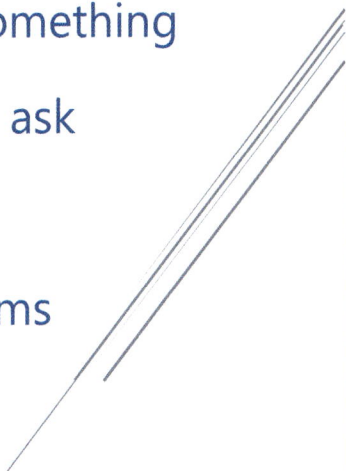

Reading is important for personal development. We have to use our imagination to flesh out the story, to create a picture of what each scene is like. As such, our version may well be different to anyone else's.

A good book allows us to have some quiet time as we become absorbed in our literary world. We have to make sense of what we're reading in ways that doesn't happen when watching a film. It's important to encourage children to read too. It supports our education, is fun and offers us an important interlude in a busy day.

A good friend will listen and be supportive
but will also know when it's time to say

'Enough!

It's time to move on'.
There comes a point where a true friend will say
'It's time to change the subject, arrange for
therapy or go and see the doctor'.
Going round in circles, talking through
the same issues can become a habit!

— ❦ —

*I love that my accountant phones and tells me when
he's coming over to do my books.
It works for me.
Discover how to motivate your clients
and provide the kind of service that
they really appreciate!*

Need to make new friends?
Get to know your neighbours.
A jar of coffee and a packet of
biscuits can be a great way to start
building new relationships.
Invite people round for an hour.

I received an email off a web designer
offering 25% off all orders placed during
the previous month!
Remember to proof read your literature.
How can potential customers trust
someone whose basic literature contains
serious mistakes!

---

*Make time for friends to chat, share,
support each other and even to
mull over the
problems of the day.
Friendships provide support
in many different ways.*

Every day brings opportunities if we remain alert.

Enjoy even the smallest of doors when they open for you.

*Approaching the second half of the year still
offers plenty of time to revisit
your resolutions, dust off those goals
and renew your resolve.
Recommit to what's*

important

for you each year.

---

*How often did you fall when you were first
learning to walk?
You kept on trying, picking yourself up each time
you fell, persevering until you succeeded.
Tap into that determination and apply it…*

today!

Buy a bunch of flowers and put them somewhere unexpected, like the kitchen, bathroom or hallway.

Little treats remind you that
YOU ARE WORTH IT.

A Mintel report reveals that 50% of Americans aged 20-30 **can't be bothered** to eat cereal for breakfast because it requires **too much effort.** They don't want to have to wash the spoon and bowl. Wonder how they feel about a Sunday roast dinner! Teach your children about the relevance of breakfast and how it's an important way to kick-start their energy for the coming day.

— ◦∙◦❀◦∙◦ —

• • •

Remember,
a high-jumper only knows
they've achieved their maximum
when they fail; otherwise they
keep raising the bar!

Set your bar
high enough to
s-t-r-e-t-c-h
you.

When surveyed, over half of the over 45's replied that getting divorced was the key to their renewed happiness, bringing with it relief, new energy and a sense of freedom. Is it time for you to make that decision or are there ways you could still re-inspire your marriage? Might caring, compassion, compromise and co-operation work and improve the quality of your relationship?

— ❦ —

It's worth spending even a few minutes each day working on your business, planning and seeing the bigger picture. Keep your hand in and stay in touch, even for a short amount of time.

— ❦ —

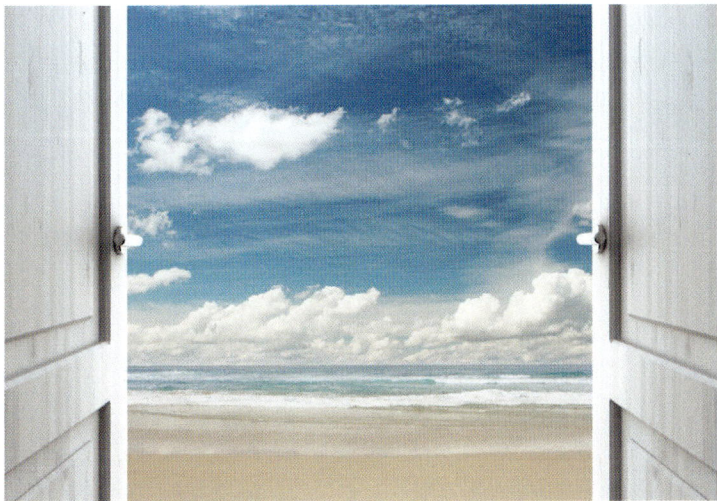

Demonstrate a readiness to listen, a desire to encourage others to share and participate.
That way they'll grow in confidence, feel involved and become an enthusiastic part of your team.
It's not all about you!

.

Be generous.

Others may struggle with things that you find easy. But equally they may breeze through things that you find tough. Learn to support each other and be strong together.

Early for a meeting?
Why not pop into a lovely hotel for coffee?
Make the most of opportunities for a break
and a little treat!

Spend time outside each day. 10 minutes in the park or on the beach just enjoying nature can ground your energy and blow away the cobwebs.

Learn to recognise your personal warning
signs that you're stressed and need some

'me time'.

Irritability, poor concentration, restless sleep,
loss of sense of humour, comfort eating are
all clues that you need a break,
a breather.

Establish yourself as the 'go to' guy,
happy to recommend others, becoming
the person others turn to when they need
to find good contacts. That way you
become the first person they
think of calling!

Is this glass
half full or
half empty?
The choice is
yours!

Used well, lists can be a great way to declutter your life, clear your mind and motivate you.
And when you do extra, you could add those items to the list too, so you can tell yourself,

'Well done!'

—— ⁂ ——

Some people spend the whole year eagerly awaiting their holidays.
Avoid being that person who puts their life on hold for a fortnight's break every few months.
Ensure your quality of life is good all year round.

Give away smiles.

*They're **free** and use less energy than frowning.* ☹

Be ready and willing to give compliments
and praise, no strings attached. A clear
'Great job! Well done! You're amazing'
can make all the difference
to someone else's day.

— ⚬⚬⚬⚬⚬ —

Stop for 10 minutes on the drive home to listen to
music, relax and have a breather.
Draw a line under the

stresses and cares

of the day and notice how you return
home with a calmer, more receptive
frame of mind.

Enjoy delicious, non-fattening ways to treat and reward yourself. Sit in the park with a book, relax in a bubble bath using those candles you've been saving for a special occasion, allow time for a long phone call with a friend or arrange a game of golf.

How often are you grateful?

It's easy to forget how fortunate we are

with our freedom, lifestyle and the things

we take for granted.

Cultivate a thankful approach to life.

— ⚬⚬⚬⚬⚬⚬ —

Keep a 'Happy Book' and make a note of three
good things that happen to you each day; a
beautiful sunset, a kindness or a little success
or achievement.
Then whenever you're feeling
blue you can look back and smile as you
recall those positive times.

Spend time with your old photographs and laugh and cry as you remember people, places and events from times gone by.

Reflect on how

f-a-r

you've come.

— ⸙ —

How many of us really know our neighbours?
We may share pleasantries, take in parcels,
pay the window cleaner, but how much do
we really know about each other?
Are we so busy that our paths rarely cross?
Invest a little time into those relationships.

Got a complaint?
Be nice to start with; it makes for
a less stressful, more positive
approach to fixing the problem.
And then you often find that
everyone's happy to help!

Holidays can put a strain on your relationship. Research shows that within a 2 week period the average British couples:

- consume 56 drinks,
- have rows 4 times,
- complain about being too hot 8 times,
- spend 2 1/2 hours a day on their mobiles,
- read 2 1/2 books.
- Added to that, 27% say they've no time to get intimate!

Discuss how to spend your time or another holiday may be needed when you get home!

—— ❦ ——

An angry customer may swear, shout and scream; they won't remember their own bad behaviour, only the way in which you treated them!

Step outside your comfort zone a little every day: it doesn't have to be radical, just enough to remind yourself that you're alive! Choose something different to eat, walk some of the way rather than ride or agree to have a go at something new. Shake up your thinking a little.

Sometimes the detours are the best, most interesting part of the journey!

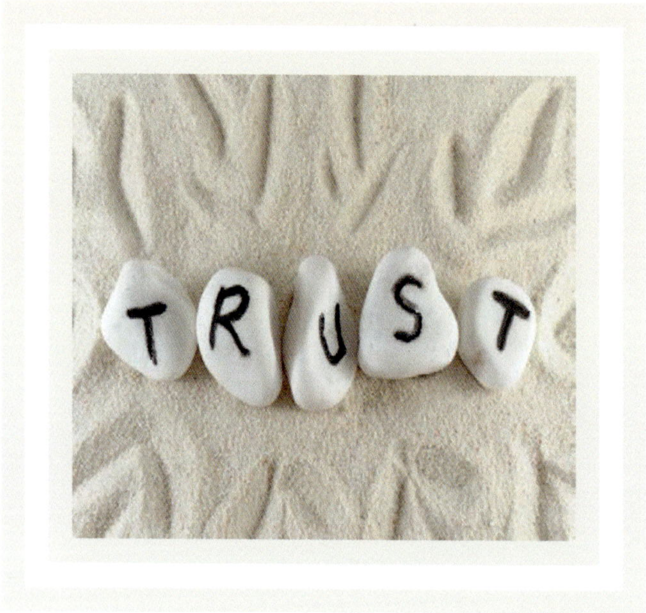
TRUST

Commit

*to your impossible goal
and marvel at how often fate,
God, the Universe come
together and the
impossible
becomes*
possible.

Use case histories and examples to illustrate

your message. Often people value hearing

about adversity, challenges overcome

and eventual success.

It's a powerful way

to humanise your story and engage

with others much more effectively.

Guess what Dame Judy Dench's 81st birthday present was from her daughter - her first tattoo, Carpe Diem inscribed on her wrist. Seize the day is apparently her motto.

Do YOU take opportunities to seize each day?

#YOLO

About the Author

As a highly respected counsellor and hypnotherapist, Susan has been helping people to transform their lives for many years. She set up Lifestyle Therapy Counselling and Hypnotherapy with her late husband and her practice is based in Altrincham, South Manchester.

Susan works with individuals, helping them to cope better with stress and the pressures of daily life; with couples to provide relationship counselling and improve communications; and in business to provide support to management, staff members and teams. She is also a highly regarded hypnotherapy trainer and public speaker.

Susan is a regular contributor to national and local BBC radio stations, including BBC Radio 5 Live and has appeared on BBC Breakfast. She also writes regularly

• • •

for many local, national and international websites and publications including The Huffington Post, as well as several business, women's and fitness magazines.

Prior to working as a counsellor and hypnotherapist, Susan worked for many years with a blue chip company and has experienced the stresses of balancing a corporate and personal life.

Susan qualified with the Academy of Curative Hypnotherapy, holds the Counselling Advanced Level 4 Diploma, is an accredited member of the Stress Management Society, Member of the Hypnotherapy Association and a Member of the National Council for Hypnotherapy (Accredited). She is registered with the Complementary and Natural Healthcare Council (CNHC) and is a member of the College of Medicine.

Contact Susan

Visit her websites: www.susanleigh.net and
www.lifestyletherapy.net

Email Susan at susan@susanleigh.net

Like the Susan Leigh Lifestyle Therapy page

Follow Susan on Twitter @SusanLeigh1